SEVEN SCRIPTURES
TO SUCCESS

SEVEN SCRIPTURES TO SUCCESS

ANTHONY ECCLESIASTES

Ecclesiastes International Publishing

First Published in 2015
by Ecclesiastes International Publishing
P.O. Box 2014
Bellingham, Washington 98227

AnthonyEcclessiastes.com

Printed in the United States of America

ISBN 978-0-692-37641-6 (paperback)
ISBN 978-0-692-39156-3 (ebook)

This book will also be available in ebook format.
For more information, please visit:
AnthonyEcclessiastes.com
or contact the author at
gatheringtheharvest@yahoo.com

Cover concept | Matt Lintz
Editor | Kendra Langeteig
Photography | Bonnie Bitz
Illustrations | Jonita Johnson, Zion Ecclesiastes, Colby Schnackenberg
Design & Typography | Kathleen Weisel (weiselcreative.com)

Note on Scripture References
All Scripture quotations in this book
are taken from The New King James Version of the Bible.

This book is dedicated in loving memory to my mother Betty Sue Westbrook and my sister Karen (Fields) White for their love and support, and also in memory of Dr. Myles Monroe for his influence early on in my ministry.

Know that God is always ready to
move on your behalf. There is no
timeout with God.

– Anthony Ecclesiastes

ACKNOWLEDGEMENTS

I give honor and glory to my Lord and Savior Jesus. I thank Him for giving me the words and wisdom to scribe **Seven Scriptures to Success**. These seven scriptures convey the completeness of His word. It is His perfect blueprint to achieving your vision and mission. I thank God for using me in this hour of revelation and power to set forth men, women, boys and girls into their destiny and purpose. I give thanks with a grateful heart.

Special Thanks

- To Abba: May your oil be poured out on those who read and dare to obey the plan laid out in this book.
- To my wife Christina Ecclesiastes, the good thing I have found for helping me to go forth.
- To my quiver full of children, beautiful blessings and inheritance from the Lord: Ki Ki Marie, Ariana, Chephren, Ephraim, Josiah, Zion, Israel, and Enoch; God-daughter Ajanae, grandchildren D'Andre and Zaden. Also thanks to the Westbrook and Hunter families.
- To Father Everett for sharing enlightenment.
- To my church family, Gathering the Harvest Tabernacle.
- To my friends in ministry around the world.
- To my editor Kendra Langeteig for her encouragement and being a great wordsmith.
- To Scarlet Ponder for Spanish translation and editing.
- To the harvest of God who will reap mightily from the life plan laid out in this book.

All profits from this book will be donated to Christ Children Character Development (CCCD), a nonprofit organization founded to support the publication of the children's book series, *The Adventures of Zion the Lion and Israel the Lamb.*

These books will stimulate the hearts and minds of your children (ages newborn to 5) to see Christ. Children and adults of all ages will fall in love with the adorable anointed characters, Zion the Lion, Israel the Lamb, Ari the Dove, and Enoch the Eagle. We thank you for your generous support of this God-given plan to edify our children.

CONTENTS

FOREWORD

When asked to write the foreword to *Seven Scriptures to Success*, the revelation knowledge you now hold in your hand, I was honored and humbled. Apostle Anthony Ecclesiastes is truly a chosen vessel of the Lord who speaks the heart of God and declares His Word with miracles, signs, and wonders following. His intimate relationship with our Father is similar to that of Enoch as shared in the Scriptures. He is a true man of prayer, faith, compassion, and passion for gathering the harvest.

Apostle Anthony has written a divinely inspired tool for health, wealth, and abundance according to "God's Perfect Blueprint" for His sons and daughters. *Seven Scriptures to Success* is written in a clear, precise, and to the point manner that provides biblical wisdom for healing and deliverance. It will stimulate every reader to achieve God success!

Seven Scriptures to Success has supernaturally inspired and changed my life! I believe it will transform the lives of all who apply the daily practices so one may see the intended result—the successful life of God's plan for each of us. With the illustration of Elisha and the widow's oil, from 2 Kings 4:1-7, Apostle Anthony clearly demonstrates that God will move you into your purpose and destiny if you apply His Word. God's anointing oil removes burdens, destroys every yoke... empowers you to be a vessel God can use to perform miracles.

Get ready to be anointed for success. As you heed the divinely inspired *Seven Scriptures to Success,* you are guaranteed to receive your miracle.

I believe in miracles!

–Apostle Kathryn Alexander, Alabaster Box International Ministries

God has called you to work
miracles, receive miracles, and to
be a miracle.

– Anthony Ecclesiastes

INTRODUCTION

GOD'S PERFECT PLAN OF ACTION

A certain woman of the wives of the sons of the prophets cried out to Elisha, saying, "Your servant my husband is dead, and you know that your servant feared the LORD. AND THE CREDITOR IS COMING TO TAKE MY TWO SONS TO BE HIS SLAVES."

²So Elisha said to her, "What shall I do for you? Tell me, what do you have in the house?" And she said, "Your maidservant has nothing in the house but a jar of oil."

³Then he said, "Go, borrow vessels from everywhere, from all your neighbors—empty vessels; do not gather just a few. ⁴And when you have come in, you shall shut the door behind you and your sons; then pour it into all those vessels, and set aside the full ones."

⁵So she went from him and shut the door behind her and her sons, who brought *the vessels* to her; and she poured *it* out. ⁶Now it came to pass, when the vessels were full, that she said to her son, "Bring me another vessel."

And he said to her, *"There is* not another vessel." So the oil ceased. ⁷Then she came and told the man of God. And he said, "Go, sell the oil and pay your debt; and you *and* your sons live on the rest." – **2 Kings 4:1-7**

"Come listen to a story about a man named Jed
A poor mountaineer, barely kept his family fed,
Then one day he was shootin' at some food,
And up from the ground came a bubblin' crude.
Oil that is, black gold, Texas tea.
Well the first thing you know ol' Jed's a millionaire,
His kinfolk said, 'Jed, move away from there!'

They said, 'Californy is the place you oughta be.'
So, they loaded up the truck and moved to Beverly.
Hills, that is, Swimmin' pools, movie stars"

(theme song from *The Beverly Hillbillies*)

You may be wondering why I put song lyrics from *The Beverly Hillbillies* alongside the seven scriptures that inspired this book. Let me explain. There are interesting parallels between the story of Jed Clampett and the story of the widow woman. Jed and the widow were both poor and attempting to keep their families fed, desperate to get relief from their situation. They both found a product to take them out of poverty into great wealth. The product was oil. This is where the similarities end. In the poor mountaineer's case, the product was crude oil. In the poor widow woman's case, the product was anointing oil. Jed discovered his oil by accident, whereas the widow woman discovered her oil by intentional prayer. Jed received a stroke of luck while out hunting one day and became a wealthy man, a multimillionaire. The widow woman received and followed the plan of God and became wealthy beyond measure in her mind, body, soul, spirit and finance.

Instead of black gold, God wants to give you spiritual gold that will lead to wealth. Instead of finding Texas tea, God wants you to drink from the fountain of heavenly tea. "Blessed are those who hunger and thirst for righteousness, for they shall be filled" (**Matthew 5:6**).

If you heed the widow's story, God will move you into your purpose and destiny. You will find your dwelling not with the movies stars but with "the bright and Morning Star" (**Revelation 22:16**).

The story of the widow's oil in these seven scriptures teaches us the lesson of how a person can go from rags to riches, poverty to prosperity, and lack to abundance. God's Perfect Blueprint for health, wealth and abundance is given to us in these **Seven Scriptures to Success**. A blueprint is a detailed plan of how to do something. The widow's story is God's blueprint for how to achieve and stay in glorious success. We will explore in detail the message conveyed in verses **2 Kings 4:1-7** for *the glory of God's Kingdom and the prosperity of His people. It is truly God's good pleasure to give us the Kingdom (***Luke 12:32***). Let your Kingdom come and your will be done (***Matthew 6:10***).*

I want to share with you the story of how this miraculous blueprint came into my hands. In March of 2012, I was invited to speak at Alabaster Box Ministries International in Los Angeles. God kept pressing upon me to preach the story of the Widow's Oil. I recall I was not feeling very well in my body and going through one of the most tremendous trials of my life. I really did not know if I was going to make it. Family, ministry, health and finances were all under attack. God gave me these seven scriptures to hold on to. I thought that this message was intended for the people I was ministering to, but it was meant for me as well. I was delivered and freed by this powerful plan of action. Little did I know that I had not received the deeper meaning of this incredible story of deliverance. Only the Word of God can deliver and nothing else under the sun can be relied on. God would never leave me alone regarding this miraculous story. He mandated me to write this book and declared that it would be a blessing of breakthrough to all who read it and applied the principles He reveals through it.

I hesitated to write this book for several reasons. One reason in particular stood out to me: I felt unworthy of such a noble assignment. God spoke to me and said: "Do not be concerned about your worthiness. It is my worthiness that I have placed inside of you." At that moment I was fine, because I had heard from the Lord. Yet I continued to procrastinate and put this God given assignment on the back shelf. Even though I had started this book, I had not sat down to work on it for a long while. I pretended that other things were more important, such as struggling through life and ministry for the Lord. I was only fooling and robbing myself of the blessings God had in store for me.

Then one day, as I was walking down the street, I heard the Lord speak to me in an audible voice. He said, "You will call this book *Seven Scriptures to Success*." I was stunned. First of all, I thought that God had forgotten about my assignment or moved on to use someone else. I realized that God never forgets and He will always hang with you even in your most foolish disposition. When I heard His voice, I laughed within myself and said, "Lord, I do not feel that I am successful. How can I write a book about success?" Then the Lord spoke again and said, "You mean to tell me that you belong to me and do not feel successful? All of heaven and earth is at your disposal. I have chosen you for a reason. Now do what I have called you to do." I was immediately delivered from my distorted view of who I was in Him. That is why this book is now in your hands.

Now God had my undivided attention and began to pour into me the substance of this book. In the following chapters, I share powerful keys inspired by the seven scriptures to help you successfully achieve the plan of God for your life. Please pay close attention to the quoted scripture verse in each chapter as it relates to the keys given.

Please Know that God Is in the Problem-Solving Business

The story of the widow's oil in 2 Kings 4:1-7 speaks of some of the great problems in life that cause much distress.

There are three major problems I would like us to take a close look at: Grief, Debt, and Bondage. Trouble seldom comes alone, but often comes in a group of woes (death of family members, financial ruin, health problems). This is true in the case of the widow woman and the trials of Job, and this may be true with the problems you face in your own life.

1. **The problem of grief**. A poor woman, widow of one of "the sons of the prophets," cried to Elisha, **"Your servant my husband is dead."** This woman's husband had recently died. She had to face the difficulties and fight the battles of life alone. Death is of one of the great tragedies of life. Death is little thought of, but common to all of us. Bereavement is the period of grief and mourning after a death. The widow woman was in deep mourning. She grieved mentally, physically, emotionally, and spiritually. Grief is part of the normal process of reacting to a painful loss of a loved one, career, home or difficult change of circumstances.

"The last enemy *that* will be destroyed *is* death... O Death, where is your sting? O Hades, where is your victory?" (**1 Corinthians 15: 26, 55**). We must understand that we have victory over death in all that we do or say. "Death and life are in the power of the tongue, and those who love it will eat its fruit" (**Proverbs 18:21**). It is up to us to walk in this fact of God and speak forth life. In the scriptures Jesus shows He is a Comforter. "Blessed are those who mourn, for they shall be comforted" (**Matthew 5:4**).

In her grief and anguish, the widow was desperate for a solution to her dilemma and she needed an answer *immediately*. She turned to the giver of all life for an answer to her grief. Jesus said, "I am the way, the truth, and the life. No one comes to the Father except through Me (**John 14:6**). No matter how hard the trials of life are, God will always make a way when it seems to be no way.

Prepare yourself, overcome grief and receive abundant life by applying the *Seven Scriptures to Success*.

2. **The problem of debt**. Her husband had been God-fearing—"**and you know that your servant feared the LORD.**" The husband's financial affairs had been left unresolved at his death, and, having no means of subsistence, the family had sunk into dependence. The husband was a good man, and yet, his sudden death brought forth adversity and reduced them from affluence to poverty. It is a sad thing when the head of a household dies and leaves to his family struggling in debt. In the seven scriptures God shows Himself as the provider. "And my God shall supply all your need according to His riches in glory by Christ Jesus" (**Philippians 4:19**). God provides money through miracle. Money is very necessary to rid ourselves of financial debt and take care of problems in our lives. The scriptures declare: "**money answers everything**" (**Ecclesiastes 10:19**).

Brace yourself for a financial miracle by following the plan laid out in *Seven Scriptures to Success*.

3. **The problem of bondage**. The creditor to whom the debt was owed showed no mercy, and, as the law permitted, was about to take as slaves the two sons of the woman (**Leviticus 25:39**). It mattered little to the hard-hearted creditor that his debtor had "feared the Lord," and that the two sons were the only remaining comforts of the widow. Altogether, the picture is a sad one. But happily, the poor woman knew where to go with her story of grief. She remembered to turn to the "Father of the fatherless" and the "Judge of the widow" (**Psalms 68:5**), and, when every earthly avenue of help was closed, she poured her sorrows into the ear of God's prophet.

Jesus says, "Therefore if the Son makes you free, you shall be free indeed" (**John 8:36**).

Get ready to receive freedom from the problems in your life by applying the wisdom in *Seven Scriptures to Success*.

May God bless you on your glorious journey to success!

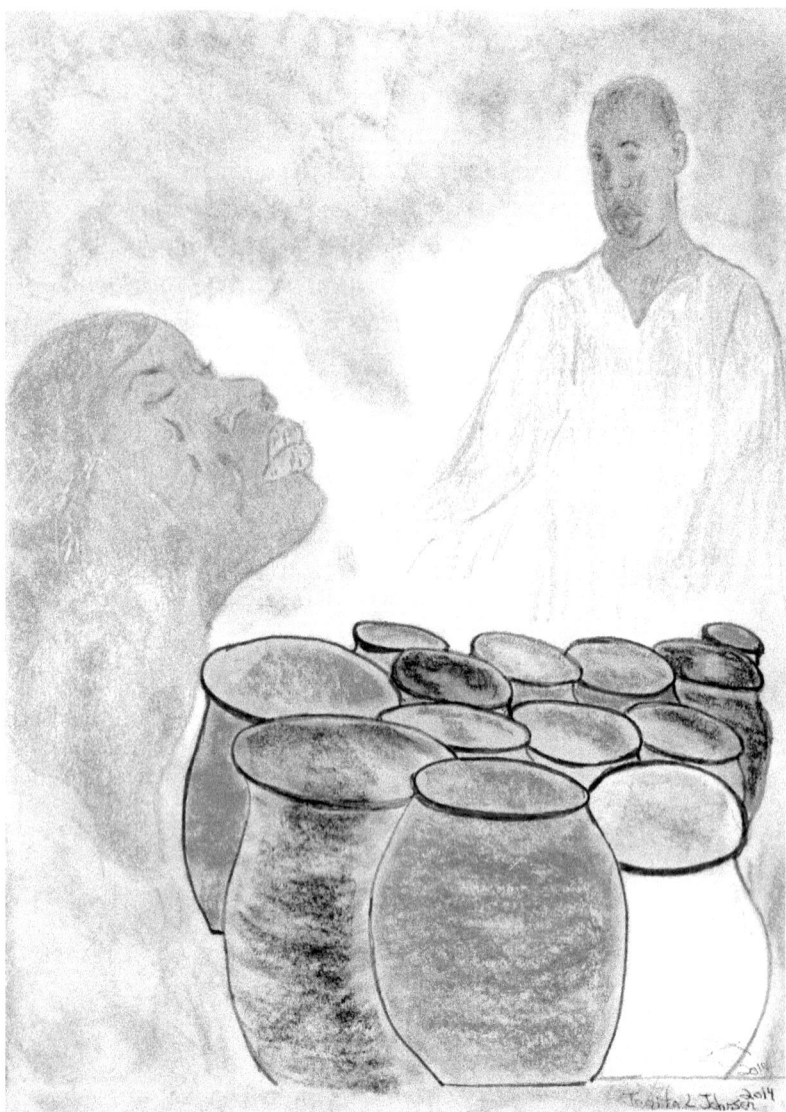

Artwork by Pastor Jonita Johnson, inspired by *Seven Scriptures to Success*. This picture demonstrates the desperation and grief of the widow woman as she prays to the prophet Elisha for a plan of help.

CHAPTER ONE

Keys to Overcoming Adversity

A certain woman of the wives of the sons of the prophets cried out to Elisha saying, "Your servant my husband is dead, and you know that your servant feared the LORD. And the creditor is coming to take my two sons to be his slaves." – 2 Kings 4:1

PRAYER COMES BEFORE POWER

Key #1) Pray to God

The woman prayed to Elisha, God's prophet, mouthpiece, and representative. The first thing you should always do is pray. Everything should be done in prayer. You are to pray without ceasing or stopping (**1 Thessalonians 5:17**). You might ask, "How can I do that?" Prayer is an attitude of gratitude. You do not necessarily have to be on your knees to pray, you can pray wherever you are. You can be driving down the street or sitting in a room filled with people and still convey an attitude of gratitude. Be very specific about what your needs and desires are. The widow woman needed deliverance from her grief and mental anguish. She suffered from the fear of losing her sons to slavery when the death of her husband put the family in financial bondage. She needed deliverance from this debt. Jesus declares: "Do not fear, little flock, for it is your Father's good pleasure to give you the kingdom (**Luke 12:32**). Just pray for what you need.

One morning I received a phone call from one of my church members who was at the hospital. He wanted me to pray for a man's 55-year-old wife who was there at the hospital. He told me that the doctors had given up on her and were going to send her home to die. The doctors said she had a bad heart and there was nothing more they could do for her. My church member put her husband on the phone. I told the husband, "We are going to pray for your wife and God is going to completely heal her." The husband said, "Yes, but the doctor said she was not going to make it." I told him we are not going to believe the doctor's report, only the report of God. We prayed and I hung up. The next morning, my member called me, and put the excited husband on the phone: "The doctors have examined my wife and they could not find anything wrong with her heart!"

Jesus says, "Whatever you ask in My name, that will I do, so that the Father may be glorified in the Son. If you ask Me anything in My name, I will do it" (**John 14:13-14**). Jesus said it, so that settles it. There is no "yes, but" about it. Just believe and do not doubt. "For assuredly, I say to you, whoever says to this mountain, 'Be removed and be cast into the sea,' and does not doubt in his heart, but believes that those things he says will be done, he will have whatever he says" (**Mark 11:23**).

FAITH NOW

Key #2) Have Faith in God

"...Faith is the substance of things hoped for, the evidence of things not seen" (**Hebrews 11:1**).

We do not walk in yesterday's faith. We do not walk in tomorrow's faith. We walk in faith NOW. Have faith in what God gives you. Faith comes by hearing the word of God (**Romans 10:17**). Jesus tells us to have faith in God (**Mark 11:22**). The woman had faith in God through the man of God Elisha. He had performed many miracles prior to his encounter with this woman. Know that God has performed many miracles prior to his encounter with you. God has a miracle for you, only just believe. The woman was very familiar with what God could do through the prophet Elisha and she trusted him. Without faith it is impossible to please God. It is the way we walk and talk. If it is not of faith it is sin. But he who doubts is condemned if he eats, because he does not eat from faith; for whatever is not from faith is sin (**Romans 14:23**).

PERSONAL RELATIONSHIP
WITH GOD

Key #3) Make Your Relationship with God Personal

We are not given the woman's name in the scriptures about the widow's oil. God calls her a "certain" woman. The world calls her a widow woman. The woman was facing the trial of her life. If we want God to move on our behalf, it is important that we take ownership of scripture and his designed plan for our life by knowing that our relationship with Him is intimate and personal. We can do this by "casting all your care upon Him, for He cares for you" (**1 Peter 5:7**). God displays certainty. The world always displays uncertainties. **Certain** means to know for sure; established beyond doubt, specific but not explicitly named or stated. Know that God has established you and specifically cares about what challenges you are facing. Each of us has a **personal relationship** with God. He cares for each and every one us more than anything or anyone in the world. He places no one above you. You are the apple of His eye (**Psalms 17:8; Proverbs 7:2**). God is constantly mindful of you and never stops thinking about you. He is in a serious relationship with us (**Psalms 8:4-6**). He so committed to you that he promises he will never leave you. "But the very hairs of your head are all numbered. Do not fear therefore; you are of more value than many sparrows" (**Luke 12:7**). God in His infinite wisdom intentionally leaves the widow's name out of the story so we all can personally relate to the story.

God wants you to place your name in the plan. Make this plan personal by applying it to your current situation or circumstances. Write your name here:

_____ (a certain man's name)
_____ (a certain woman's name).

Know that you are established beyond doubt. "For I know the thoughts that I think toward you, says the Lord, thoughts of peace and not of evil, to give you a future and a hope" (**Jeremiah 29:11**). Embrace this miracle plan as yours, because it *is* yours.

Key #4) Respect God

"The fear of the Lord is the beginning of wisdom, and the knowledge of the Holy One is understanding" (**Proverbs 9:10**). This scripture tells us that the woman's husband feared the Lord. This means that he reverenced and respected the Lord and he passed this reverence (fear) on to his wife and children. Will you walk in reverence to God?

The widow's husband left her the rich inheritance of the Word of God. Believe His word and you will never walk in failure.

Key #5) Possess Character

Her husband was a son of the prophets. He sat under the tutelage of Elisha, just as we sit under the teachings of Jesus: "For as many as are led by the Spirit of God, these are sons of God" (**Romans 8:14**). To be led by God's spirit is to put on the nine attributes of His Spirit: "But the fruit of the Spirit is love, joy, peace, longsuffering, kindness, goodness, faithfulness, gentleness, self-control. Against such there is no law" (**Galatians 5:22-23**).

A Good Man

"A good man leaves an inheritance for his children's children and the wealth of the wicked is stored up for the just" (**Proverbs 13:2**).

The dead prophet left a living inheritance of respect and character for the widow and her sons to glean from. The widow woman had just lost her husband whom she loved dearly. He was a wonderful man of God and a part of a group of prophets that was headed up by the prophet Elisha, who received a double portion of the anointing from his mentor Elijah. The widow woman's husband heard from God and released God's word into the life of others. He had the assurance of salvation, but no insurance or apparent inheritance for his family at his death. Just about every commentary regarding this miraculous story makes the husband out to be a deadbeat dad and neglectful husband by emphasizing how he did not leave an inheritance for his family. Suddenly the widow woman was faced with overwhelming grief and an uncertain future. No longer did she have a "house band" to protect her against the wilds of society (The word husband means house band, one who bands the house together; from Middle English *huseband*, "house" + bōndi, būandi, "to dwell," "householder"). She needed God to become the one to band or hold her house together. The Lord impressed upon me the realization that the dead prophet had left a great inheritance that led to the ultimate deliverance of his family. There are three important inheritances the prophet left his family and they are as follows.

Threefold Inheritance for All of Us

1. **Inheritance of Godly Association**
   Blessed is the man
   who walks not in the counsel of the ungodly,
   nor stands in the path of sinners,
   nor sits in the seat of the scornful;
   but his delight is in the law of the Lord,
   and in His law he meditates day and night.
   He shall be like a tree
   planted by the rivers of water,
   that brings forth its fruit in its season,
   whose leaf also shall not wither;
   and whatever he does shall prosper. (**Psalms 1:1-3**)

The deceased husband was a Prophet who walked in the counsel of the Prophet Elisha. He stood in the blessings of a prophet of God, so prosperity belonged to him and his family. Because of his association with Elisha and the school of prophets, his wife knew to call on Elisha during her time of need.

2. **Inheritance of Reverence**
   The woman's testimony of her husband to Elisha was not a testimony of information but of confirmation of

who he was to her and to Elisha: "You know that your servant feared the Lord" (**2 Kings 4:1**). "The fear of the Lord is the beginning of wisdom, and the knowledge of the Holy One is understanding" (**Proverbs 9:10**). The word fear in this scripture means to reverence or respect. When reverence is present we are able to receive His knowledge and understanding.

3. **Inheritance of Oil**
   The jar of oil found in the widow's house belonged to her deceased husband. The prophet used this oil daily to minister to others. Now this very same jar of oil is being used to remove burdens and destroy yokes off the life of his family. The prophet truly left an inheritance of the Spirit and the catalyst for the miraculous, the anointing oil (**Isaiah 27:10**).

Put Relationship over Religion

The woman is a widow and her sons are fatherless. If we as the bride of Christ do not know Him (Christ) as husband, we are widowed. If we do not know God as Father, we are fatherless. God promises in His scriptures to take care of all who fall under this category, lack of relationship.

"A father of the fatherless, a defender of widows, *is* God in His holy habitation" (**Psalms 68:5**). God expects us to be the same way He is because we are made in His image and Likeness and should come after Him in all that we say or do. If He helps the widow and orphan, we should do the same. "Pure religion, undefiled before God and the Father, is this: to visit the fatherless and widows in their affliction, and to keep himself unspotted from the world" (**James 1:27**). This is the only time in scripture where the word religion is used positively; it is used with the adjective "pure" in front of it. Purity always points to

Relationship with God. "Blessed are the pure in heart: for they shall see God" (**Matthew 5:8**).

So the woman turned to God in prayer by making her request known to the man of God, Elisha, who was the mouthpiece of God, and through him she knew God would provide a solution. She did not panic but placed her trust in the hands of the Master. "Trust in the Lord with all your heart and lean not on your own understanding; in all your ways acknowledge Him and he will direct your paths" (**Proverbs 3:5, 6**). She was willing to stand still and see the salvation of the Lord. She was specific and open about her problem. We have not because we ask not. God wants us to make our request known to Him and trust Him. He is faithful in leading us out of the circumstances that life may bring. She needed protection, peace and provision. She needed a miracle.

Know that God is always ready to move on your behalf. There is no timeout with God.

The religion that God respects is relationship. We must have relationship with each other and relationship with Him. The father expects us to do for each other what he does for each one of us. This is where God lives and strives: in the taking care of His people. Jesus says: "Most assuredly, I say to you, the Son can do nothing of Himself, but what He sees the Father do; for whatever He does, the Son also does in like manner" (**John 5:19**).

I pray that there is someone reading this book today that finds themself in need: someone who is fatherless, widowed, sorrowful, poor, or destitute. I pray that you are willing to humble yourself and receive your miracle plan for your life. God has a miracle for every one of us. He will give us the Oil of Gladness to cure our sadness (**Psalms 45:7**).

CHAPTER TWO

What's in Your House?

**So Elisha said to her, what shall I do for you?
What do you have in the house? And she said,
your maidservant has nothing in the house
but a jar of oil. – 2 Kings 4:2**

Key #6) Answer God's Questions

When God asks us, **"What shall I do for you?"** you must be very ready to answer Him. Don't be afraid to be desperate with God. You know you need it and He is the provider of all things (**Philippians 4:19**). Blurt it out, spill the beans. Stop trying to be cute with God. Let the tears and snot flow freely. He loves the undignified, one that will become completely open and honest with Him. Let us face it; you cannot fool God, so why even try. "Call to Me, and I will answer you, and show you great and mighty things, which you do not know" (**Jeremiah 33:3**). Tell Him you need a plan.

Key #7) Know What You Possess

God inquired as to her possessions, **"What do you have in the house?"** God has gifted and equipped every man to carry out a plan of success. God takes His starting-point from what we already have. The widow had but "**a jar of oil**," oil for anointing; but this was made the basis of what was to be done. So Elijah founded his miracle on the widow of Zarephath's "handful of meal in a barrel, and a little oil in a cruse" (**1 Kings 17:12**), and with Moses, his "rod." "So the Lord said to him, 'What *is* that in your hand?' He said, 'A rod.' And He said, 'Cast it on the ground.' So he cast it on the ground, and it became a serpent; and Moses fled from it. Then the Lord said to Moses, 'Reach out your hand and take *it* by the tail' (and he reached out his hand and caught it, and it became a rod in his hand), that they may believe that the Lord God of their fathers, the God of Abraham, the God of Isaac, and the God of Jacob, has appeared to you" (**Exodus 4:2-5**).

God wants to use what we already possess. In other words, He wants to put His super on our natural. He will supernaturally use you with what you already have. Do not despise small beginnings (**Zechariah 4:10**). Start with what you have.

Key #8) Trust in the Holy Spirit

"Trust in the Lord with all your heart, and lean not on your own understanding; in all your ways acknowledge Him, And He shall direct your paths" (**Proverbs 3:5-6**).

"Your maidservant has nothing in the house but a jar of oil."

Just when you think you have nothing, know that you have something that God can use. Nothing was left but a small jar of anointing oil, but that bit of oil was sufficient. God used it powerfully to demonstrate His Spirit: "'Not by might nor by power, but by My Spirit,' says the Lord of hosts" (**Zechariah 4:6**).

Embodiment

The jar of oil is a picture of the embodiment of Holy Spirit. Embodiment means the representation or expression of something in a tangible or visible form. We are made in the image and likeness of God: "In the image of God He created him; male and female He created them" (**Genesis 1:27**). When God made Adam He saw Himself in the mirror, His very image. God then breathed His Spirit into the man. "And the Lord God formed man of the dust of the ground, and breathed into his nostrils the breath of life; and man became a living being" (**Genesis 2:7**). It has always been God's desire to fill His vessels with His Spirit: "for in Him we live and move and have our being, as also some of your own poets have said, for we are also His offspring" (**Acts 17:28**).

Precious Oil Is the Presentation of His Spirit

> It shall come to pass in that day, that his burden will be taken away from your shoulder, and his yoke from your neck and the yoke will be destroyed because of **the anointing oil**. (**Isaiah 10:27**)

Yes, that is right. Burdens are being removed and yokes are being destroyed because of **the anointing oil.** Jesus is the anointing oil spoken of in this scripture. Jesus is the burden removing, yoke-destroying power of God mentioned in Isaiah 10:27. Ladies and gentleman, I introduce to you the anointing oil Jesus! "How God **anointed** Jesus of Nazareth with the Holy Spirit and with power, who went about doing good and healing all who were oppressed by the devil, for God was with Him" (**Acts 10:38**).

Oil Is Everything, Just Like Jesus

> The Spirit of the Lord is upon Me, because He has anointed Me to preach the gospel to the poor; He has sent Me to heal the brokenhearted, to proclaim liberty to the captives, and recovery of sight to the blind, to set at liberty those who are oppressed; to proclaim the acceptable year of the Lord. – **Luke 4:18-19**

This scripture passage from Luke covers the spiritual side of what we are empowered to do when we are anointed like Jesus with the Spirit of the Lord (oil). Almost every time the bible mentions oil, it is referring to olive oil. Oil that was pressed from the fruit of olive trees had many uses in biblical times. It was a dietary staple. It was spread on bread, used for cooking, and mixed with flour to make bread.

Oil was used as a spiritual offering (**Leviticus 2:4**), as a remedy for stomach distress and as a balm to heal wounds. It was also used as a fuel for lamps in homes. Soldiers often worked oil into the leather shields they used in battle. This kept the shields from becoming brittle.

Oil was also the base for making perfumes and fragrant ointments. When perfumers boiled oil and then added secret blends of root and bark powders, tree resins, and spices, they could make very expensive ointment. One jar of oil-based myrrh, frankincense, cinnamon and aloe ointment could sell for as much as one laborer's yearly salary.

Oil was a precious item in international trade. Solomon had traded it years before to pay for supplies he used to build the temple (**2 Chronicles 2:10**).

When the widow told Elisha what had happened, he instructed her to sell the oil and pay off her husband's debts. The woman and her sons were then able to live on the money that was left over. Truly God provided Elisha as a friend to this family in their time of need.

GOD CAN USE YOU!

Know that we always have something God can use to deliver us and others. He gives to every man a measure of Time, Talent, and Treasure. You are never left destitute no matter how bad the circumstances may appear. What has God given you? Perhaps you have an ideal, a vision, money, love, compassion, wisdom, passion, or an assignment. You name it. Whatever it is, He can use it to deliver you.

The widow woman replied that she had nothing of value "**but a jar of oil**." It appeared to have no value to her, but God instructed Elisha to give her a plan of action according to what she possessed. It was a small flask of anointing oil. She said, I have nothing left except for the anointing, a small skin of oil. The root word used in Hebrew is "asuk," which means "anointed." It is the anointing that removes every burden and destroys every yoke. The Prophet also left an inheritance of power: "It shall come to pass in that day that his burden will be taken away from your shoulder, and his yoke from your neck, and the yoke will be destroyed because of the anointing oil" (**Isaiah 10:27**).

This tiny portion of oil was more than enough and God used it mightily. It was a presentation of the person of the Holy Spirit. The small flask of oil was anointed to saturate every vessel it came in contact with. As long as there are vessels, the anointing will flow. We are called to saturate the world with our anointing: "Spirit of the Lord is upon me, He has anointed me" (**Luke 4:18**). Preach, heal, free, release, and recover.

This woman was in need of a plan. She was captive because of her financial situation. If you are not financially free, you are not free. She was blind as to what to do and needed instruction. She was brokenhearted from her loss. She was in search of liberty from certain bondage for her sons. Do you have anything the Lord can use? Identify your jar of oil and use it.

CHAPTER THREE

Borrow Vessels

Then he said, Go, borrow vessels from everywhere, from your neighbors – empty vessels, do not gather just a few. – 2 Kings 4:3

YOU ARE COMMISSIONED

Key #9) Go

The verb "go" in Hebrew is "yalak," which means to walk. In this scripture the verb *go* is used as a command. God is ready for you to walk into your destiny and blessings. God has always been ready. The question is, are you ready? This is urgent business. God wants to meet our need: "And my God shall supply all your need according to His riches in glory by Christ Jesus" (**Philippians 4:19**).

The scripture verse 2 Kings 4:3 quoted above parallels the **Great Commission**: "Then the eleven disciples went away into Galilee, to the mountain which Jesus had appointed for them. When they saw Him, they worshiped Him; but some doubted. And Jesus came and spoke to them, saying, "All authority has been given to Me in heaven and on earth. Go therefore and make disciples of all the nations, baptizing them in the name of the Father and of the Son and of the Holy Spirit, teaching them to observe all things that I have commanded you; and lo, I am with you always, *even* to the end of the age" (**Matthew 28:16-20**). Amen.

The disciples did not go right away; because of doubt and fear many just went back to their houses and resumed their normal life. They hesitated to follow the plan Jesus laid out for them. It was not until persecution closed in that they began to move. "As for Saul, he made havoc of the church, entering every house, and dragging off men and women, committing them to prison. Therefore those who were scattered went everywhere preaching the word" (**Acts 8:3-8**). Do not wait to do what God has given you to do now. Go! Do not procrastinate. Procrastination is the action of delaying or postponing something. Get started now.

Key #10) Borrow

Elisha taught the woman and her sons to "borrow not a few" empty vessels. Borrowing usually has a bad reputation in scripture: "The rich rule over the poor and the borrower is servant to the lender" (**Proverbs 22:7**). When you know you are commissioned or commanded by God to achieve the end results, he wants you to be determined to get there. If he says borrow, then borrow. The verb "borrow" in Hebrew is "shaal," which means, "to ask" or "beg" for something. When you really want what God has for you, you will not be shy but bold. You will not be slack but diligent. You will become that door-to-door solicitor that is so often despised by others. You will desperately **A**sk and **S**eek and **K**nock (ASK) ."**A**sk, and it shall be given you; **s**eek, and ye shall find; **k**nock, and it shall be opened unto you" (**Matthew 7: 7**). Get the vessels any way you honorably can. Get as many as possible; the more vessels, the more oil you will have. The widow was to expect large things from the Lord. Her task in collecting the vessels was a work of faith. God does not ignore us in answer to our prayers. His word rather is, "Open your mouth wide, and I will fill it" (**Psalms 81:10**). If in faith we will ask him, he will astonish us with his answers.

LOVE YOUR NEIGHBORS

Key #11) Invest in People

People are our greatest resource and they are the vessels of God, designed in His image. (The Hebrew noun for vessels is "kaliy," which means a utensil or implement or apparatus of nearly any kind.) The vessels, when filled with precious oil, are an image of the believer saturated with the Holy Spirit. "And you shall love the Lord your God with all your heart, with all your soul, with all your mind, and with all your strength." This is the first commandment. And the second, like it, is this: 'You shall **love your neighbor** as yourself.' There is no other commandment greater than these" (**Mark 12:30-31**). Jay Paul Getty made three hundred people millionaires before he became one. Invest your efforts in people and you will be blessed.

Key #12) Fill the Empty

But now, "O Lord, You are our Father; we are the clay, and You our potter; and all we are the work of Your hand" (**Isaiah 64:8**). God wants to mold us into the unique vessel He has called us to be.

"Reyq" is the Hebrew word for "empty," which means to **"pour out"** or to empty. We as vessels are to pour everything out of our lives that does not belong there. God is in search of poured out vessels so he can pour in His Holy Spirit (oil). "And it shall come to pass in the last days, says God, That I will **pour out of My Spirit on all flesh**; Your sons and your daughters shall prophesy, Your young men shall see visions, Your old men shall dream dreams" (**Acts 2:17**). We must pour out the old in order for God to pour in the new.

FILL YOUR VESSELS

Elisha commissioned the woman to go. We are also commissioned to go and spread the oil of gladness, His Spirit. "Go therefore, and teach all nations, baptizing them in the name of the Father, and of the Son, and the Holy Spirit" (**Matthew 28:19**). God wants you to walk into your destiny. He is commanding us to get started. God told the widow woman to start a home-based business with a sense of urgency. She and her sons started a door-to-door business to borrow and beg for vessels.

God wants us to touch as many vessels (people) as we can with what is in our house. The anointing was in the widow's house, the power to fill vessels until there is no more to fill. God wants us to use what He has blessed us with to deliver ourselves and others. God always expects a return on His investment. He is willing to invest in the vessels that He has made in His image and likeness. The vessels were filled with precious oil, the embodiment (the representation or expression of something in a tangible or visible form) of the believer being filled with His Holy Spirit. He invests His anointing that removes burdens and destroys yokes. He gives us a problem-solving Spirit to overcome every obstacle and remove every trial. Finally, Elisha tells the woman to borrow not a few empty vessels but get as many as possible. He commanded her to be determined (diligent) in her doing. She had to be bold and convincing in her approach. Much like preaching, she had to exhibit belief. The more vessels collected, the more the oil flowed. Everything is pointing to the fervency in gathering the vessels. Be on fire and excited when it comes to the filling of the precious Holy Spirit of God. His presence is essential in all that we do.

Follow His command. Listen to God. We hear him by responding.

God believes in you and knows you can achieve whatever you set your mind to. God is our biggest encourager. He is saying, "You can do it. I know you can."

– Anthony Ecclesiastes

CHAPTER FOUR

Trust and Obey

**And when you have come in, you shall shut the
door behind you and your sons;
then pour it into all those vessels, and set
aside the full ones. – 2 Kings 4:4**

Do not follow after your own heart and thoughts, but pay close attention to the direction of God even if you do not understand the whys of what He is doing. "There is a way *that seems* right to a man, but its end *is* the way of death" (**Proverbs 14:12**).

> Trust in the LORD WITH ALL YOUR HEART, and lean not on your own understanding; In all your ways acknowledge Him, and He shall direct your paths (**Proverbs 3:5-6**).

The widow woman trusted and acknowledged the direction of God.

Key #13) Come in

"Come to Me, all *you* who labor and are heavy laden, and I will give you rest. Take My yoke upon you and learn from Me, for I am gentle and lowly in heart, and you will find rest for your souls. For My yoke *is* easy and My burden is light" (**Matthew 11:28-30**).

Whenever God gives us a clear plan of action, distractions will always try to divert us from the mission. We must be aware of it in order to deflect opposition. Anything worth having will be a challenge. Listen very closely to God's instructions in verse 4. First we must **come** into agreement with His will. Jesus's Mother said to the servants before Jesus turned the water into wine, "whatever He says do it" (**John 2:5**).

GET FOCUSED

Key #14) Shut the door

The widow is told to do her work in private. Jesus did some of His miracles in private also. Some things are to be done with the door shut. They are just too precious and private to be shared with doubting unspiritual eyes. When God gives you a plan, do not link up with the spirit of unbelief. Jesus said in regards to the healing of Jarius's daughter: "Do not be afraid; **only believe**, and she will be made well" (**Luke 8:50**).

Stay on the Wall

We must **shut the door** to distractions. If Nehemiah had paid attention to what was going on around him in the outside world, he would never have rebuilt the walls of Jerusalem in 52 days. There were 12 different ways they attempted to pull him off the wall:

1. They laughed at him.
2. They despised him.
3. They accused him of rebellion.
4. They were furious toward him.
5. They were very indignant toward him.
6. They mocked him.
7. They said he was feeble.
8. They said he was stupid (whatever he built would fall apart).
9. They conspired against him to bring attack and confusion.
10. They threatened to kill him to stop his work.
11. They asked to meet with him to trick him and cause him harm (4 times they requested this).
12. They lied about him in a public letter to create fear and failure.

Nehemiah shut out his cares and concerns about the enemies and set his mind to working the plan of God with a sword in one hand, a hammer in the other hand, and a prayer on his lips. The widow and her sons did the same. So must we if we want to succeed.

When Jesus raised the little 12-year-old girl from the dead, He said to them, "Why make this commotion and weep? The child is not dead, but sleeping." And they ridiculed Him. **But when He had put them all outside**, He took the father and the mother of the child, and those *who were* with Him, and entered where the child was lying. Then He took the child by the hand, and said to her, "Talitha, cumi," which is translated, "Little girl, I say to you, arise." Immediately the girl arose and walked, for she was twelve years *of age*. And they were overcome with great amazement" (**Mark 5:39-42**).

On another occasion, we see the deaf man with a speech defect being healed by Jesus "aside from the multitude." "And He took him **aside from the multitude**, and put His fingers in his ears, and He spat and touched his tongue. Then, looking up to heaven, He sighed, and said to him, 'Ephphatha,' that is, 'Be opened.' Immediately his ears were opened, and the impediment of his tongue was loosed, and he spoke plainly" (**Mark 7:33-35**).

Sometimes you have to get out of the sight of people to take care of what God has called you to do. **Jesus encourages us to do in private: our praying, our giving, and our fasting.**

"Therefore, when you do a charitable deed, do not sound a trumpet before you as the hypocrites do in the synagogues and in the streets, that they may have glory from men. Assuredly, I say to you, they have their reward. But when you do a charitable deed, do not let your left hand know what your right hand is doing, that your charitable deed may be in secret; and your Father who sees in secret will Himself reward you openly" (**Matthew 6:2-4**).

Gethsemane is where Jesus prayed after the Last Supper and before his arrest and Crucifixion. The name Gethsemane originates from a Hebrew term meaning "oil press," suggesting that the garden was a grove of olive trees. This is a place where Jesus frequently went and shut the door in prayer and labor before the Father. This is why Judas knew where he would be. Gethsemane is the place of pressing in and great focus. Here Jesus refreshes Himself with a fresh infilling of the Holy Spirit (fresh oil). Elisha told the woman to shut the door. When God gives you a plan, do not let in any distraction. A lack of faith could kill your plan. You do not want people around you saying it won't work, you can't accomplish it; or saying you are too stupid, too fat, too skinny, too young, or too old. You have to shut the door and only allow in the faithful.

PERFORM THE TASK

Key #15) Pour Out

God wants every vessel of His to overflow with His Spirit, power, and abundance. God commands the widow woman to "**pour out**" into all those empty vessels. The Hebrew verb for pour, "yatzsaq," means to let flow or to overflow. "You prepare a table before me in the presence of my enemies; You anoint my head with oil; My cup runs over" (**Psalms 23:5**).

We are to **pour into** others the anointing that God has bestowed upon us. "And it shall come to pass in the last days, says God, That I will **pour out** of My Spirit on all flesh (vessels); Your sons and your daughters shall prophesy, Your young men shall see visions, Your old men shall dream dreams" (**Joel 2:28; Acts 2:17**). When they are full we can set them aside for the increased multiplication of His kingdom.

BE DEDICATED

Key #16) Set aside

God instructed the woman to "**set aside the full ones.**"

Once the vessels were filled, they were set aside to fulfill their purpose. When a vessel (the image of a believer) is completely filled with oil, a form of embodiment of the Holy Spirit, he or she can be "set aside," dedicated, consecrated, and used in a special way for the purposes of God. Consecrate means to make holy or to dedicate to a higher purpose. You must always remember you have a higher purpose. Stop trying to look like the oil of sadness of this world and put on the oil of gladness of God.

The believer should be glad to be sanctified, or set apart. **Sanctification** is a state of separation unto God; all believers enter into this state when they are born of God: "But of Him you are in Christ Jesus, who became for us wisdom from God—and righteousness and **sanctification** and redemption" (**1 Corinthians 1:30**).

It should be our heart's constant desire to be filled with the Spirit of God and be used by God. When we are full, we can be set aside for the increased multiplication of His kingdom.

CHAPTER FIVE

Be Determined

**So she went from him and shut the door
behind her and her sons, who brought her
vessels to her, and she poured it out.
– 2 Kings 4:5**

Key #17) Teamwork

God told the widow to include her sons and start an oil factory out of their home. To put this in modern day terms, it was a family-run business directed by God. She poured the oil and had meetings with the Prophet Elisha. Her sons ran public relations, inventory, and general operations. They even had a slew of investors. Together they set up a powerful distributions system. What a great staff. The woman and her two sons were truly a team at work. Just like the acronym **TEAM: Together Everyone Achieves More.**

Key # 18) Urgency

The creditors were coming and the woman and her sons did not have time to waste and neither do you. Whatever God has in mind for you, He will help you do it quickly, smoothly, and precisely. Who said it has to take a long time? You serve a "right now" God. Have a sense of **urgency** in regards to your God given plan. Look at it this way: "Weeping may endure for a night, but joy comes in the morning" (**Psalms 30:5**). This is an exact description of the miracle in the *Seven Scriptures to Success.*

OBEDIENCE IS BETTER THAN SACRIFICE

Key #19) Obey

The Woman did exactly what she was told. She obeyed the commands of the prophet. The prophet said, "Go," and she went. Elisha also said to borrow vessels, shut her door, and include her sons, and she did. Then he commanded her to pour the oil and she poured until there were no more vessels to fill. She did all that was commanded of her. What great **obedience**. "If you are willing and obedient, you shall eat the good of the land" (**Isaiah 1:19-20**).

Invest what you have to make an increase. Do not hold back, but pour it all out to create more. Do not be afraid of losing the little bit that you have. Be willing to let go of what is in your possession so that you may receive more. Remember, what you currently possess is not going to meet your need. God wants us to be willing cheerful givers. The widow woman believed God and achieved great results. She was willing to pour out all that she had to gain what she needed. She poured out so that more would be poured in.

My 8-year-old son Zion's interpretation of the widow's story in *Seven Scriptures to Success*. The woman prays and God fills her with oil (Holy Spirit) as a vessel of God.

CHAPTER SIX

Be a Chosen Vessel

**Now it came to pass when the vessels were
full, that she said to her son, "Bring me
another vessel." – 2 Kings 4:6**

Before Paul was in relationship with God, he was
caught up in religion and wanted to kill everyone and
everything that opposed his beliefs. Then God met Paul
one day and changed his heart. Ananias heard about this
hard-hearted religious man and believed there was no
hope for him, but God reassured Ananias and said these
words to him in regard to Paul: "But the Lord said to him,
"Go, for he is a **chosen vessel** of Mine to bear My name
before Gentiles, kings, and the children of Israel" (**Acts
9:15**). "And Ananias went his way and entered the house;
and laying his hands on him he said, "Brother Saul, the
Lord Jesus, who appeared to you on the road as you came,
has sent me that you may receive your sight and be filled
with the Holy Spirit (oil)" (**Acts 9:17**). God consistently
refers to us in his word as vessels. We are vessels for
honor, sanctified (set apart) and useful for the Master,
prepared for every good work (**2 Timothy 2:21**).

Key #20) Multiply Your Oil

The Oil Multiplied

The widow and her sons did as directed, and as they poured the oil into the borrowed vessels, it still increased till the vessels were full. The element of miracle here is very notable. But the pledge of Divine help in distress implied in such a miracle remains to us, and God will honor every draft on his promises made in faith, basing itself on such deeds as this. It might almost be said that there is a multiplying power in the divine blessing, apart from miracle (**Psalms 37:16**).

The Oil Remained

When the vessels were full, the widow said to her son, "Bring me another vessel." There was not, however, a vessel more. Then the oil remained. Had there been more vessels, it would have flowed on. The sole limit of the supply is the limit of our capacity to receive. We are not limited in God; we are limited only in ourselves. The widow woman worked diligently because she knew that God rewards those who diligently seek Him in faith (**Hebrews 11:6**). She believed in the Plan of God and nothing was going to stop her from receiving her blessing. She stirred up the ability that was in her to create wealth by carrying out the plan to the detail. It is God's intention to fill all available vessels with His anointing and power. It should be our desire to impart into every vessel the power of God

(Holy Spirit). God cannot begin to use us until our vessels are filled with oil (Holy Spirit).

The Oil Sold

The news being brought to Elisha, he ordered the grateful woman (poor no more) to sell the oil, and pay her debt, and live with her children on the rest. The debt was not forgiven; it was paid. God puts His stamp of approval on honesty. The whole incident teaches us the lesson of trusting God in every time of need. When have the righteous been forsaken, or their seed seen begging bread? (**Psalms 37:25**). If we can trust in God for temporal supplies, much more may we trust in God for our spiritual supplies (**Philippians 4:19**).

As long as there were empty vessels, the oil flowed and was not exhausted. The supply never ended. The insufficiency was on the vessel end, the human end, not the supply end of the miracle. If they gathered more empty vessels, they would have had more oil to fill them. The oil, being an image of the Holy Spirit, was absolutely inexhaustible. Just as the oil was more than enough, the Holy Spirit is more than sufficient in our lives.

Illustration by artist Colby Schnackenberg. This picture shows the victory of the widow woman and her family as they come out of poverty into prosperity. They are able to sell the oil and live on the rest.

CHAPTER SEVEN

Pathway to Prosperity

And he said to her, 'There is not another vessel.' So the oil ceased. Then she came and told the man of God. And he said 'Go sell the oil and pay your debt, and you and your sons live on the rest.' – 2 Kings 4:7

The oil of God will cease when there are no more vessels to fill. As long as there are vessels there will be oil. God is always looking for a vessel He can use and set apart for His glory and honor. God gave three directives in verse 7: 1) Go sell, 2) Go pay, and 3) Go Live. Let us examine each of these directives.

Key #21) Go Sell

Sell means to give or hand over something in exchange for money. Many of us would walk away if God told us to become salesmen. We'd say, "No thanks Lord, I want a pay check." But a paycheck will limit the plan of God for your life. There will always be a ceiling to how much you can actually receive financially with a paycheck. A paycheck is always connected to a job, j-o-b (just over broke), or a boss telling you how much you are worth. There is no limitation to what you are worth. A job will never pay you what you are worth, and even if it paid a lot, it would never be able to afford you. You are fearfully and wonderfully made. You are the head and not the tail. You are above and not beneath. You bless in the city and bless in the field. You bless going in and going out. There is no limit to what you can do. You are a miracle waiting to happen. Take your miracle plan and go to the realm of overflowing blessings just like the woman and her sons. Another word for sell is promote. Promote your product that is the Holy Spirit in **you**. You are God's greatest resource. Sell your oil.

Key #22) Go Pay Your Debt

It is only right to pay one's debts. Many of us would spend until there is no more left and file Chapter 11, ending up broke, busted, and disgusted all over again. "Owe no one anything except to love one another, for he who loves another has fulfilled the law" (**Romans 13:8**). Don't get a bad reputation and ruin a good testimony over delinquent debts. If you can't pay something on time, call the company and explain the situation and work out a plan of some kind. They will usually cooperate with any sincere client.

she borrowed and boost the economy of her community with her newly founded oil business. The provision God made enabled the widow woman to obtain and maintain financial freedom well into her future and beyond.

In the story of the widow's oil, we see a fulfilled and happy woman with two sons rejoicing in the things of God. The "income" of the Holy Spirit will pay the "debts" of the believer.

We are often told not to get our
hopes up. We are encouraged to
have REALISTIC expectations.
God wants us to have MIRACLE
expectations. Expect a lot
from the Lord!

– Anthony Ecclesiastes

CHAPTER EIGHT

Miracles Can Be Yours

There are many kinds of vessels to fill to the brim with oil—large ones, small ones, tall ones, short ones, different colored ones (white, black, brown, red) pretty ones, ugly ones. These vessels have one thing in common: a God who cares about their welfare. Regardless of their differences, they all have great value because of the spiritual oil that is inside of them.

Do you have any oil in your house? Is your vessel filled to the brim and spilling over into the lives of others? Is it worth enough to get you out of debt? Can it save the lives of you and your family? Can it provide a future? The answer is *Yes, Lord*.

This is a time of miracles. We have endless gallons of oil being produced instantly (without the aid of the olive tree), a process that normally takes months. This reminds me of Jesus' miracle of turning water into wine. A large quantity of fine wine was produced immediately without the assistance of grape vines, rain, sunshine and time. God wants to perform an immediate miracle in your life in a short period of time.

This widow woman exchanged want for wealth and poverty for plenty. You can have a miracle in your life soon.

I BELIEVE IN MIRACLES

It was the summer of 1960 in the sweltering heat of the deep south of Savannah, Georgia. A 16-year-old frightened girl by the name of Betty Sue had come to the harsh reality that she was two months pregnant. Betty Sue had been without a mother or father since the age of seven. She lived an insecure life between aunts' houses and various relatives. Betty Sue was afraid to tell those who loved her she was with child, so she turned to a mysterious old woman for advice about her pregnancy. Little did Betty Sue know that this mysterious old woman practiced "root doctoring," or Hoodoo. This is an African American folk magic tradition that was developed over several centuries in the Southern United States.

The old woman convinced Betty Sue to drink a potion mixed with turpentine oil, a resinous extract from pine trees. This oil is poisonous to the human body and should never be orally consumed. The old witch assured her this oil would abort the pregnancy and no one would ever know she had been pregnant. Betty Sue became very sick, but the baby remained attached to her body to full term, born on Saint Patrick's Day, March 17, 1961. Betty Sue had a son and named him Anthony. Her son was weak and frail. The doctors predicted he would not live to see the age of 13. Betty Sue loved her baby and resolved in her mind that her child would live.

Betty Sue and her son moved to the New England state of Massachusetts. It was here that she became very involved with the Church of God in Christ. Although much prayer went forth, Betty Sue's son remained very ill as a consequence of the turpentine oil.

One cold blistery winter evening while at home in their

tiny apartment, the toll of son's illness had run its course and the child, now 4 years of age, stopped breathing. Her baby was dead. The 21-year-old mother did not panic but took her child and wrapped him in a blanket and carried him three miles through the cold wintery streets of Springfield, Massachusetts to the home of a praying married couple, Brother and Sister Bayman. They were members of her church.

She unwrapped her son's already cold and blue body and requested prayer. They prayed fervently and the breath of life returned to her son's body. He was raised from the dead and never experienced another day of sickness.

I am the son of this frightened, unwed teenage mother who once turned to a witch that spoke death by Turpentine Oil, and who later turned to saints that spoke life back into me by the Oil of Gladness (Jesus).

More than 50 years later, I am alive to write **Seven Scriptures to Success** and release the miraculous power of God into your life. I am a miracle and God has a miracle for you.

YOU NEED A MIRACLE

A **Miracle** is a surprising and welcome event that is not explicable by natural or scientific laws and is therefore considered to be the work of a divine agency. A Miracle is also an amazing product or achievement, or an outstanding example of something.

God can give you the miracle of oil, too, just like He did for the widow woman in His miraculous perfect plan of action.

And you, like the widow, can be associated with the "Oil of Gladness," the precious Holy Spirit of God! God uses that very term in prophesying about Jesus in Psalms: "You love righteousness and hate wickedness; Therefore God, Your God, has anointed You with the **oil of gladness** more than Your companions" (**Psalms 45:7**).

MIRACLE MULTIPLICATION

Miracle multiplication is nothing like the math we learned in school. School math is based on fact, not on faith. But Miracle math is based on faith over fact. Can I ask you a question? Do you need a miracle in your life? So many people do not believe in miracles, but miracles are happening around us every day.

Just recently, one of my church members was shot four times, at point blank range, by an intruder in his home as he went to answer the front door. The doctors did not think he was going to make it. I went to visit him every day for a week. When he was still in a coma, I anointed him with oil daily and prayed the prayer of Faith. The Lord spoke this word in regards to him: "You shall live and not die. You will be better, stronger than you were before." I just kept praying the word that God gave while he remained unconscious.

When he came out of the coma after three days, I spoke this word to him: "'You shall live and not die. You will be better, stronger than you were before." The scriptures, saturated in oil, continued to bless this whole man and he recovered. He is now healthier stronger and better than he was before the shooting. I have laid hands on those who had cancer and they recovered. I expect miracles to happen.

When oil is poured and rubbed upon your vessel, it begins to spread and penetrate into your skin and nourish the tissue and beyond. When we consume the oil orally on a consistent basis, it becomes connected to your vessel.

The vessel takes on the characteristics of what it contains.

YOU ARE A MIRACLE WORKER

God has called you to work miracles, receive miracles, and to be a miracle. *Seven Scriptures to Success* is about the miraculous power of God. You have the power of God. "Now God worked **unusual miracles** by the hands of Paul, so that even handkerchiefs or aprons were brought from his body to the sick, and the diseases left them and the evil spirits went out of them" (**Acts 19:11**). God is not a respecter of person. If He uses Paul, He will use you. In the seven scripture about the widow woman, God uses the prophet Elisha. Elisha was a well-known miracle worker who showed the desperate woman how to become a miracle worker, just as his mentor Elijah had shown him. Elisha received a double portion of the anointing (oil) and was able to perform twice the Miracles of his mentor, and master Elijah, as you see in the list of miracles on the following pages.

Miracles in the Career of Elisha (Elijah's disciple)

1) Parting of the Jordan (2 Kings 2:14)

2) Healing of the waters (2 Kings 2:21)

3) Curse of the she bears (2 Kings 2:24)

4) Filling of the valley with water (2 Kings 3:17)

5) Deception of the Moabites with the valley of blood (2 Kings 3:22)

6) **Miracle of the vessels of oil (2 Kings 4:4)**

7) Prophecy that the Shunammite woman would have a son (2 Kings 4:16)

8) Resurrection of the Shunammite's son (2 Kings 4:34)

9) Healing of the gourds (2 Kings 4:41)

10) Miracle of the bread (2 Kings 4:43)

11) Healing of Naaman (2 Kings 5:14)

12) Perception of Gehazi's transgression (2 Kings 5:26)

13) Cursing Gehazi with leprosy (2 Kings 5:27)

14) Floating of the axe head (2 Kings 6:6)

15) Prophecy of the Syrian battle plans (2 Kings 6:9)

16) Vision of the chariots (2 Kings 6:17)

17) Smiting the Syrian army with blindness (2 Kings 6:18)

18) Restoring the sight of the Syrian army (2 Kings 6:20)

19) Prophecy of the end of the great famine (2 Kings 7:1)

20) Prophecy that the scoffing nobleman would see, but not partake of, the abundance (2 Kings 7:2)

21) Deception of the Syrians with the sound of chariots (2 Kings 7:6)

22) Prophecy of the seven-year famine (2 Kings 8:1)

23) Prophecy of Benhadad's untimely death (2 Kings 8:10)

24) Prophecy of Hazael's cruelty to Israel (2 Kings 8:12)

25) Prophecy that Jehu would smite the house of Ahab (2 Kings 9:7)

26) Prophecy that Joash would smite the Syrians at Aphek (2 Kings 13:17)

27) Prophecy that Joash would smite Syria thrice but not consume it (2 Kings 13:19)

28) Resurrection of the man touched by his bones (2 Kings 13:21)

Prophet Elijah's Miracles

1) Causing the rain the cease for 3 ½ years (1 Kings 17:1)

2) Being fed by the ravens (1 Kings 17:4)

3) Miracle of the barrel of meal and cruse of oil (1 Kings 17:14)

4) Resurrection of the widow's son (1 Kings 17:22)

5) Calling of fire from heaven on the altar (1Kings 8:38)

6) Causing it to rain (1 Kings 18:45)

7) Prophecy that Ahab's sons would all be destroyed (1 Kings 21:22)

8) Prophecy that Jezebel would be eaten by dogs (1 Kings 21:23)

9) Prophecy that Ahaziah would die of his illness (2 Kings 1:4)

10) Calling fire from heaven upon the first 50 soldiers (2 Kings 1:10)

11) Calling fire from heaven upon the second 50 soldiers (2 Kings 1:12)

12) Parting of the Jordan (2 Kings 2:8)

13) **Prophecy that Elisha should have a double portion of his spirit (2 Kings 2:10)**

14) Being caught up to heaven in a whirlwind (2 Kings 2:11)

Now God will show you in *Seven Scriptures to Success* how to press in to the miracle plan for your life. The great miracle worker Jesus said: "Most assuredly, I say to you, he who believes in Me, the works that I do he will do also; and greater works than these he will do, because I go to My Father" (**John 14:12**).

God is challenging you to
overcome unimportant opinions
and get on with your plan of
action. God will take even the
smallest effort and have it grow
into something large.

– Anthony Ecclesiastes

CHAPTER NINE

What Is Success?

See your goal

    Understand the obstacles

        Create a positive mental picture

          Clear your mind of self-doubt

            Embrace the challenge

              Stay on track

                Show the world you can do it

**Success is the effect of sound wisdom,
the accomplishment of an aim or purpose.**

Solomon the Successful Wise King

Solomon was the wisest man who ever lived, the very symbol of wisdom. He was able to build the house of the Lord and his own house, as well as pen Proverbs and the book of Ecclesiastes. He asked for success at a young age to rule and reign over the people, and the Lord was so impressed with his request that he gave him success (wisdom), riches and long life (**1 Kings 3:6-15**).

BE A BUILDER

Thus Solomon finished the house of the LORD and the king's house; and Solomon **successfully accomplished all** that came into his heart to make in the house of the LORD and in his own house (**2 Chronicles 7:11**).

GET SUCCESS

"If the ax is dull, and one does not sharpen the edge, then he must use more strength; **but wisdom brings success**" (**Ecclesiastes 10:10**). Wisdom is the principal thing, therefore get wisdom.

"And in all your getting, get understanding" (**Proverbs 4:7**). Get wisdom (success). When we labor in the natural it is hard. God has called us to labor in the supernatural (Holy Spirit). "His yoke is easy and His burden is light" (**Matthew 11:30**).

Joshua the Successful Leader

"This Book of the Law shall not depart from **your mouth**, but **you shall meditate** in it day and night, that you may observe to **do according** to all that is written in it. For then **you will make your way prosperous,** and then **you will have good success**" (**Joshua 1:8**).

HOW TO HAVE SUCCESS

1. **Speak the Word** – But He answered and said, "It is written, 'Man shall not live by bread alone, but by every word that proceeds from the mouth of God'" (**Matthew 4:4**).

2. **Meditate on the Word** – "Finally, brethren, whatever things are true, whatever things are noble, whatever things are just, whatever things are pure, whatever things are lovely, whatever things are of good report, if there is any virtue and if there is anything praiseworthy, meditate on these things" (**Philippians 4:8**).

3. **Do the Word** – "But be doers of the word, and not hearers only, deceiving yourselves" (**James 1:8**).

   Results: **You will live a prosperous life.**
   You will have good success.

Joshua needed encouragement as the new leader of God's people. So the Lord gave him sound instruction to achieve success. Joshua, which is the Hebrew word for Jesus (salvation), did not deviate from this instruction and he accomplished all his goals. By the end of the book of Joshua, he uttered these words. "And if it seems evil to you to serve the Lord, choose for yourselves this day whom you will serve, whether the gods which your fathers served that were on the other side of the river, or the gods of the Amorites, in whose land you dwell. But as for me and my house, we will serve the Lord" (**Joshua 24:15**).

Success is the ability to know how to lead and follow. Joshua followed the word of God and successfully led God's people to victory in the Promised Land. Follow the teaching in *Seven Scriptures to Success* and win the promised victory for your life.

BE AN ACCOMPLISHED PERSON

Success is the effect of sound wisdom, the accomplishment of an aim or purpose. We have all heard the term used in reference to someone who has accomplished something. This meaning speaks to what we have done or what we stand for. God has mandated me to pour the oil of this book into every vessel until there are no more vessels to fill; to help all who read it accomplish great things by applying the substance of *Seven Scriptures to Success.* Study this powerful God given book and receive His guaranteed freedom and success.

CHAPTER TEN

Significance of the Book Title

While walking my Siberian husky on the shores of Bellingham Bay, God spoke to me that each word of the title is of great importance. I will explain the meaning of these words so that you can appreciate their significance.

Scriptures Are the Inspired Word of God

The word "scripture" is used 51 times in the New Covenant, always with reference to the *Holy Scripture.*

In biblical scripture, there are two Greek words that God would like to bring to your attention: *Logos* and *Rhema.* I will explain their significance here.

LOGOS

Logos is the total inspired Word of God, the word or principle of divine reason and creative order, identified in the Gospel of John with the second person of the trinity incarnate in Jesus Christ.

The following passages of Scripture give examples of the *logos* of God:

"In the beginning was the Word, and the Word was with God, and the Word was God" (**John 1:1**).

"The seed is the word of God" (**Luke 8:11**).

"Holding forth the word of life" (**Philippians 2:16**).

"Be diligent to present yourself approved to God, a worker who does not need to be ashamed, rightly dividing the word of truth" (**II Timothy 2:15**).

"For the word of God is quick, and powerful" (**Hebrews 4:12**).

"Being born again, not of corruptible seed, but of incorruptible, by the word of God, which lives and abides forever" (**I Peter 1:23**).

RHEMA

The second primary Greek word that describes Scripture is **Rhema**, which refers to a word that is spoken and means "an utterance." A rhema is a verse or portion of Scripture that the Holy Spirit brings to our attention with application to a current situation or need for direction.

Every word of God is inspired, and "all scripture is given by inspiration of God, and is profitable for doctrine, for reproof, for correction, for instruction in righteousness" (**II Timothy 3:16**). It is the Holy Spirit who illuminates particular Scriptures for application in our daily walk with the Lord.

The words of Jesus are significant on this point. "Man shall not live by bread alone, but by every word (rhema) that proceeds out of the mouth of God" (**Matthew 4:4**). Jesus also stated: "The words (rhema) that I speak unto you, they are spirit, and they are life" (**John 6:63**).

When God's spirit speaks to us through a word or scripture, He expects us to act upon it.

God spoke to me a rhema that lines up with the logos to pour into your life the oil of *Seven Scriptures to Success,* just as the widow woman poured oil into each vessel she received. God in His infinite wisdom decided to reveal His Perfect plan in seven scriptures in **2 Kings 4:1-7**.

Seven Is God's Perfect and Complete Number

In Scripture, seven symbolizes completeness or perfection.

On the seventh day, God rested from his labors and creation is finished (**Genesis 2:2**).

Pharaoh in his dream saw seven cattle coming from the Nile (**Genesis 41:2**).

Samson's sacred Nasserite locks were braided in seven plaits (**Judges 16:13**).

Seven devils left Mary of Magdalene, signifying the totality of her previous possession by Satan (**Luke 8:2**); "seven other devils" will enter the purified but vacant life of a person (**Matthew 12:45**). However, on the positive side, there were the seven spirits of God (**Revelation 3:1**).

In the seventh year, the Hebrew slave was to be freed, having completed his time of captivity and service (**Exodus 21:2**).

Every seventh year was a sabbatical year (**Leviticus 25:4**).

Seven times seven reiterates the sense of completeness. In the Year of Jubilee (at the completion of 7 x 7 years = the 50th year), all land is freed and returns to the original owners (**Leviticus 25:10**). Pentecost, the Feast of Weeks, is seven times seven days after Passover.

"Seventy," which is "sevens" in Hebrew, strengthens the concept of perfection. There are 70 elders in Israel (**Exodus 24:1**). Israel was exiled to Babylon for 70 years (to complete its punishment (**Jeremiah 25:12**). "Seventy times seven" reiterates this further (**Matthew 18:22**). The Lord was not giving Peter a mathematical number of times that he should forgive another person, but rather was insisting on limitless forgiveness for a brother's sin.

Seven is God's number of perfection and completion in both the physical and spiritual aspects of life. Right at the start of the Bible, the number 7 is identified with something being "finished" or "complete." From then on, that association continues, as 7 is often found in contexts involving completeness or divine perfection. If you are not acknowledging this spiritual truth, you are not walking in the completeness and perfection of who you are called to be. Jesus is our life and He and the Father come to us in completeness and perfection in the person of Holy Spirit.

Seven derives much of its meaning from being directly tied to God's creation of all things. According to Hebrew history, the creation of Adam took place on October 7th, 3761 B.C. or on the 1st day of Tishri the seventh month of the Hebrew calendar. The word "created" is used seven times in the illustration of God's creative work in **Genesis 1:1, 21,27** and **Genesis 2:3, 2:4**.

Our week cycle is 7 days and God's Sabbath is on the 7th day. The bible has seven major categories: 1) The Law; 2) The Prophets; 3) The writings of David and Solomon; 4) The Gospels and Acts; 5) The writings of Paul; 6) The other Epistles; and 7) The book of Revelation.

There are seven men in the first covenant referred to as Man of God: Moses (**Joshua 14:6**); David (**2 Chronicles 8:14**); Samuel (**1 Samuel 9:6, 14**); Shemaiah (**1 Kings 12:22**); Elijah (**1 Kings 17:18**); Elisha (**2 Kings 5:8**); and Igdaliah (**Jeremiah 35: 4**).

In the book of **Hebrews**, there are seven descriptions ascribed to Jesus (Christ); they are as follows: "Heir of all things" (**1:2**); "Captain of Salvation" (**2:10**); "Apostle" (**3:1**); "Author of Salvation" (**5:9**); "Forerunner" (**6:20**); "Priest" (**10:21**); and "Author and Finisher of Our Faith" (**12:2**).

In the thirteen chapter of the book of Matthew, Jesus gives seven powerful parables (**Matthew 13:3-9, 24-30, 31-32, 33, 44, 45-46, 47**). Seven psalms are ascribed to David in the New Covenant (**Psalms 2, 16, 32, 41, 69, 95 and 109**).

In the book of Revelation, there are seven churches, seven angels to the seven churches, seven seals, seven trumpet plagues, seven thunders and the seven last plagues. The first resurrection of the dead takes place at the seventh trumpet, completing the salvation for the Church.

The number seven is also linked to the seven annual Holy Days, starting with Passover and completing with the Feast of Tabernacles in the fall. The cycle of the Holy days (where we get the word holidays) is completed in three festival seasons by the 7th month of the sacred calendar: Passover and Unleavened Bread, 1st month; Pentecost, 3rd month; and Trumpets, Atonement, Tabernacles and Last Great Day, in the 7th month.

The 7 Miracles of Jesus on the 7th Day

Jesus performed seven miracles on God's holy Sabbath Day (which ran from Friday sunset to Saturday sunset). Here are the seven Miracles and their symbolic meaning as they apply to your own life.

1. Jesus healed the withered hand of a man attending church service (**Matthew 12:9**). God will restore all good things that have withered away from your life.

2. At a Capernaum Church He casts out an unclean spirit that possessed a man (**Mark 1:21**). God will cast out every unclean thing that would stop you from fulfilling your purpose.

3. Jesus heals Peter's Mother in Law of a fever in Peter's House (**Mark 1:29**). God will remove every manner of disease from your House (body) and use you for His glory.

4. A woman attending church, who was made sick by a demon for eighteen years, is released from her bondage (**Luke 13:11**). God will remove all the bondages that hold you back no matter how long they have been present.

5. At a Pharisee's house eating a meal with the host and several Lawyers, Jesus heals a man with dropsy (**Luke 14:2**). God will heal you in the midst of your detractors and people who think they are better or greater than you are.

6. A man who is disabled and unable to walk is healed at the pool of Bethesda (**John 5:8-9**). God will enable you to walk into your destiny.

7. Jesus heals a man born blind at the pool of Siloam (**John 9:14**). God will restore your vision and send you into your destiny.

God does not view seven as a lucky number, but He sees it as His significant number of completion, perfection. God in His infinite wisdom decided to reveal His Perfect plan in seven scriptures in 2 Kings 4:1-7.

God uses seven scriptures in 2 Kings 4:1-7 to demonstrate the completion and perfection of His word for our life. Please enjoy these lessons and apply God's perfect plan to your life.

CHAPTER ELEVEN

Daily Practice – Scriptures on the Power of Anointing Oil

The 40 scriptures in this chapter regard the power of anointing with oil. Choose one to read each day to prime and refresh your spirit.

Exodus 29:7 – And you shall take the anointing oil, pour *it* on his head, and anoint him.

Exodus 29:36 – And you shall offer a bull every day *as* a sin offering for atonement. You shall cleanse the altar when you make atonement for it, and you shall anoint it to sanctify it.

Exodus 30:25-30 – And you shall make from these a holy anointing oil, an ointment compounded according to the art of the perfumer. It shall be holy anointing oil. [26] With it you shall anoint the tabernacle of meeting and the ark of the Testimony; [27] the table and all its utensils, the lampstand and its utensils, and the altar of incense; [28] the altar of burnt offering with all its utensils, and the laver and its base. [29] You shall consecrate them, that they may be most holy; whatever touches them must be holy. [30] And you shall anoint Aaron and his sons, and consecrate them, that *they* may minister to Me as priests.

Exodus 30:30 – And you shall anoint Aaron and his sons, and consecrate them, that *they* may minister to Me as priests.

Exodus 40:9 – And you shall take the anointing oil, and anoint the tabernacle and all that *is* in it; and you shall hallow it and all its utensils, and it shall be holy.

Leviticus 6:20 – *This is* the offering of Aaron and his sons, which they shall offer to the LORD, *beginning* on the day when he is anointed: one-tenth of an ephah of fine flour as a daily grain offering, half of it in the morning and half of it at night.

Leviticus 8:12 – And he poured some of the anointing oil on Aaron's head and anointed him, to consecrate him.

Ruth 3:3 – Therefore wash yourself and anoint yourself, put on your *best* garment and go down to the threshing floor; *but* do not make yourself known to the man until he has finished eating and drinking.

1 Samuel 15:1 – Samuel also said to Saul, "The LORD sent me to anoint you king over His people, over Israel. Now therefore, heed the voice of the words of the LORD."

1 Samuel 16:13 – Then Samuel took the horn of oil and anointed him in the midst of his brothers; and the Spirit of the LORD came upon David from that day forward. So Samuel arose and went to Ramah.

2 Samuel 2:4 – Then the men of Judah came, and there they anointed David king over the house of Judah. And they told David, saying, "The men of Jabesh Gilead *were the ones* who buried Saul."

2 Samuel 5:3 – Therefore all the elders of Israel came to the king at Hebron, and King David made a covenant with them at Hebron before the LORD. And they anointed David king over Israel.

1 Kings 1:39 – Then Zadok the priest took a horn of oil from the tabernacle and anointed Solomon. And they blew the horn, and all the people said, "*Long* live King Solomon!"

1 Kings 19:16 – Also you shall anoint Jehu the son of Nimshi *as* king over Israel. And Elisha the son of Shaphat of Abel Meholah you shall anoint *as* prophet in your place.

2 Kings 9:3 – Then take the flask of oil, and pour *it* on his head, and say, "Thus says the LORD: 'I have anointed you king over Israel.' Then open the door and flee, and do not delay."

2 Kings 9:6 – Then he arose and went into the house. And he poured the oil on his head, and said to him, "Thus says the LORD God of Israel: 'I have anointed you king over the people of the LORD, over Israel.'"

2 Kings 11:12 – And he brought out the king's son, put the crown on him, and *gave him* the Testimony; they made him king and anointed him, and they clapped their hands and said, "Long live the king!"

Psalms 23:1-6 – The LORD *IS* MY SHEPHERD;
I shall not want.
² He makes me to lie down in green pastures;
He leads me beside the still waters.
³ He restores my soul;
He leads me in the paths of righteousness
For His name's sake.

⁴ Yea, though I walk through the valley of the shadow of death,
I will fear no evil;
For You *are* with me;
Your rod and Your staff, they comfort me.

⁵ You prepare a table before me in the presence of my enemies;
You anoint my head with oil;
My cup runs over.
⁶ Surely goodness and mercy shall follow me
All the days of my life;
And I will dwell in the house of the LORD
Forever.

Psalms 45:7 –
You love righteousness and hate wickedness;
Therefore God, Your God, has anointed You
With the oil of gladness.

Isaiah 61:1 – The Spirit of the Lord GOD *IS* UPON ME,
Because the LORD HAS ANOINTED ME
To preach good tidings to the poor;
He has sent Me to heal the brokenhearted,
To proclaim liberty to the captives,
And the opening of the prison to *those who are* bound.

Isaiah 61:3 – To console those who mourn in Zion,
To give them beauty for ashes,
The oil of joy for mourning,
The garment of praise for the spirit of heaviness;
That they may be called trees of righteousness,
The planting of the LORD, THAT HE MAY BE GLORIFIED.

Matthew 6:17 – But you, when you fast, anoint your head and wash your face

Matthew 26:6-13 – And when Jesus was in Bethany at the house of Simon the leper, [7] a woman came to Him having an alabaster flask of very costly fragrant oil, and she poured *it* on His head as He sat *at the table.* [8] But when His disciples saw *it,* they were indignant, saying, "Why this waste? [9] For this fragrant oil might have been sold for much and given to *the* poor."

[10] But when Jesus was aware of *it,* He said to them, "Why do you trouble the woman? For she has done a good work for Me. [11] For you have the poor with you always, but Me you do not have always. [12] For in pouring this fragrant oil on My body, she did *it* for My burial. [13] Assuredly, I say to you, wherever this gospel is preached in the whole world, what this woman has done will also be told as a memorial to her."

Mark 6:13 – And they cast out many demons, and anointed with oil many who were sick, and healed *them.*

Mark 14:8 – She has done what she could. She has come beforehand to anoint My body for burial.

Mark 16:1 – Now when the Sabbath was past, Mary Magdalene, Mary *the mother* of James, and Salome bought spices, that they might come and anoint Him.

Luke 4:18-19 – The Spirit of the Lord is upon Me,
Because He has anointed Me
To preach the gospel to the poor;
He has sent Me to heal the brokenhearted,
To proclaim liberty to the captives
And recovery of sight to the blind,
To set at liberty those who are oppressed;
To proclaim the acceptable year of the Lord.

Luke 7:38 – And stood at His feet behind *Him* weeping; and she began to wash His feet with her tears, and wiped *them* with the hair of her head; and she kissed His feet and anointed *them* with the fragrant oil.

Luke 7:46 – You did not anoint My head with oil, but this woman has anointed My feet with fragrant oil.

Luke 10:33-34 – [33] But a certain Samaritan, as he journeyed, came where he was. And when he saw him, he had compassion. [34] So he went to him and bandaged his wounds, pouring on oil and wine; and he set him on his own animal, brought him to an inn, and took care of him.

John 11:2 – It was *that* Mary who anointed the Lord with fragrant oil and wiped His feet with her hair, whose brother Lazarus was sick.

John 12:3 – Then Mary took a pound of very costly oil of spikenard, anointed the feet of Jesus, and wiped His feet with her hair. And the house was filled with the fragrance of the oil.

Acts 2:1-47 – Coming of the Holy Spirit

When the Day of Pentecost had fully come, they were all with one accord in one place. [2] And suddenly there came a sound from heaven, as of a rushing mighty wind, and it filled the whole house where they were sitting. [3] Then there appeared to them divided tongues, as of fire, and *one* sat upon each of them. [4] And they were all filled with the Holy Spirit and began to speak with other tongues, as the Spirit gave them utterance.

[5] And there were dwelling in Jerusalem Jews, devout men, from every nation under heaven. [6] And when this sound occurred, the multitude came together, and were confused, because everyone heard them speak in his own language.

[7]Then they were all amazed and marveled, saying to one another, "Look, are not all these who speak Galileans? [8]And how *is it that* we hear, each in our own language in which we were born? [9]Parthians and Medes and Elamites, those dwelling in Mesopotamia, Judea and Cappadocia, Pontus and Asia, [10]Phrygia and Pamphylia, Egypt and the parts of Libya adjoining Cyrene, visitors from Rome, both Jews and proselytes, [11]Cretans and Arabs—we hear them speaking in our own tongues the wonderful works of God." [12]So they were all amazed and perplexed, saying to one another, "Whatever could this mean?"

[13]Others mocking said, "They are full of new wine."

Peter's Message

[14]But Peter, standing up with the eleven, raised his voice and said to them, "Men of Judea and all who dwell in Jerusalem, let this be known to you, and heed my words. [15]For these are not drunk, as you suppose, since it is *only* the third hour of the day. [16]But this is what was spoken by the prophet Joel:

[17]'And it shall come to pass in the last days, says God,
That I will pour out of My Spirit on all flesh;
Your sons and your daughters shall prophesy,
Your young men shall see visions,
Your old men shall dream dreams.
[18]And on My menservants and on My maidservants
I will pour out My Spirit in those days;
And they shall prophesy.
[19]I will show wonders in heaven above
And signs in the earth beneath:
Blood and fire and vapor of smoke.
[20]The sun shall be turned into darkness,
And the moon into blood,

Before the coming of the great and awesome day of the Lord.

²¹ And it shall come to pass

That whoever calls on the name of the Lord

Shall be saved.'

²² Men of Israel, hear these words: Jesus of Nazareth, a Man attested by God to you by miracles, wonders, and signs which God did through Him in your midst, as you yourselves also know— ²³ Him, being delivered by the determined purpose and foreknowledge of God, you have taken by lawless hands, have crucified, and put to death; ²⁴ whom God raised up, having loosed the pains of death, because it was not possible that He should be held by it. ²⁵ For David says concerning Him:

"I foresaw the Lord ALWAYS BEFORE MY FACE,

For He is at my right hand, that I may not be shaken.

²⁶ Therefore my heart rejoiced, and my tongue was glad;

Moreover my flesh also will rest in hope.

²⁷ For You will not leave my soul in Hades,

Nor will You allow Your Holy One to see corruption.

²⁸ You have made known to me the ways of life;

You will make me full of joy in Your presence."

²⁹ Men *and* brethren, let *me* speak freely to you of the patriarch David that he is both dead and buried, and his tomb is with us to this day. ³⁰ Therefore, being a prophet, and knowing that God had sworn with an oath to him that of the fruit of his body, according to the flesh, He would raise up the Christ to sit on his throne, ³¹ he, foreseeing this, spoke concerning the resurrection of the Christ, that His soul was not left in Hades, nor did His flesh see corruption. ³² This Jesus God has raised up, of which we are all witnesses. ³³ therefore being exalted to the right hand of God, and having received from the Father the promise of the Holy Spirit, He poured out this which you now see and hear.

[34] For David did not ascend into the heavens, but he says himself:

"The LORD SAID TO MY LORD,

Sit at My right hand,

[35] Till I make Your enemies Your footstool."

[36] "Therefore let all the house of Israel know assuredly that God has made this Jesus, whom you crucified, both Lord and Christ."

[37] Now when they heard *this,* they were cut to the heart, and said to Peter and the rest of the apostles, "Men *and* brethren, what shall we do?"

[38] Then Peter said to them, "Repent, and let every one of you be baptized in the name of Jesus Christ for the remission of sins; and you shall receive the gift of the Holy Spirit. [39] For the promise is to you and to your children, and to all who are afar off, as many as the Lord our God will call."

[40] And with many other words he testified and exhorted them, saying, "Be saved from this perverse generation." [41] Then those who gladly received his word were baptized; and that day about three thousand souls were added *to them.* [42] And they continued steadfastly in the apostles' doctrine and fellowship, in the breaking of bread, and in prayers. [43] Then fear came upon every soul, and many wonders and signs were done through the apostles. [44] Now all who believed were together, and had all things in common, [45] and sold their possessions and goods, and divided them among all, as anyone had need.

[46] So continuing daily with one accord in the temple, and breaking bread from house to house, they ate their food with gladness and simplicity of heart, [47] praising God and having favor with all the people. And the Lord added to the church daily those who were being saved.

Acts 4:27 – For truly against Your holy Servant Jesus, whom You anointed, both Herod and Pontius Pilate, with the Gentiles and the people of Israel, were gathered together.

Acts 10:38 – how God anointed Jesus of Nazareth with the Holy Spirit and with power, who went about doing good and healing all who were oppressed by the devil, for God was with Him.

2 Corinthians 1:21-22 – Now He who establishes us with you in Christ and has anointed us is God, who also has sealed us and given us the Spirit in our hearts as a guarantee.

Hebrews 1:9 – You have loved righteousness and hated lawlessness; Therefore God, Your God, has anointed You With the oil of gladness more than Your companions.

James 5:13-16 – [13] Is anyone among you suffering? Let him pray. Is anyone cheerful? Let him sing psalms. [14] Is anyone among you sick? Let him call for the elders of the church, and let them pray over him, anointing him with oil in the name of the Lord. [15] And the prayer of faith will save the sick, and the Lord will raise him up. And if he has committed sins, he will be forgiven. [16] Confess your trespasses to one another, and pray for one another, that you may be healed. The effective, fervent prayer of a righteous man avails much.

1 John 2:20 – But you have an anointing from the Holy One, and you know all things.

1 John 2:27 - But the anointing which you have received from Him abides in you, and you do not need that anyone teach you; but as the same anointing teaches you concerning all things, and is true, and is not a lie, and just as it has taught you, you will abide in Him.

CHAPTER TWELVE

Blueprint for Your Miracle of Success

I can do all things through Christ who strengthens me. – Philippians 4:13

A blueprint is a detailed plan of how to do something. If you follow the plan laid out in *Seven Scriptures to Success* and apply it to what God has given you to accomplish, you will have success in the next 40 days. This blueprint is God Guaranteed.

God believes in you and knows you can achieve whatever you set your mind to. God is our biggest encourager. He is saying, "You can do it. I know you can." We are often told not to get our hopes up. We are encouraged to have REALISTIC expectations. God wants us to have MIRACLE expectations. Expect a lot from the Lord!

The more specific you are, the better the results will be. God is challenging you to get what He has for you. The word "challenge" has some negative connotations. The meaning we are using here is, "a test of one's abilities or resources in a demanding but stimulating undertaking." We all need to be challenged from time to time. God is challenging you to overcome unimportant opinions and get on with your plan of action. God will take even the smallest effort and have it grow into something large.

The following section includes focus questions, a guide for using the 23 keys, and a questionnaire to help you create a solid plan for your miracle of success.

WRITING YOUR ACTION PLAN

Focus Questions

"Write the vision and make it plain on tablets, that he may run who reads it" (**Habakkuk 2:2**).

It is important that you write down your plan for the miracle of success you want to see happen in your life. Be so specific that if a stranger were to pick up your plan, that person would be able to use it for guidance in their own life.

1. What is the success miracle that you want God to help you accomplish? (Finance, Health, Relationship etc.)

_____

_____

_____

_____

_____

_____

_____

2. Why do you need this miracle in your life? Consult your checklist below.

_____

_____

_____

_____

_____

_____

_____

3. What do you need to do to make this miracle happen?
    List your main goals, tasks, and requirements.

    _____

    _____

    _____

    _____

    _____

    _____

    _____

4. What product(s) can you sell to bring you success?
    List your talent, skills, ideas, possessions etc. (See
    Key #7)

    _____

    _____

    _____

    _____

    _____

    _____

    _____

5. Who will be on your team to help put your plan into
    action? List personal support, professional support,
    financial support etc. (See Key #17)

    _____

    _____

    _____

    _____

    _____

    _____

    _____

6. Where will you work on your plan? (home, office location, coffee shop, school etc.)

_____

_____

_____

_____

_____

_____

_____

7. How much time will you devote each day/week/ month to put your plan into action? Create a weekly schedule. (See Keys #12 and #13)

_____

_____

_____

_____

_____

_____

_____

8. What makes you uniquely qualified to succeed? Who does God say that you are?

_____

_____

_____

_____

_____

_____

_____

9. What will you do to keep faith in your miracle plan and be successful in 40 days?

_____

_____

_____

_____

_____

_____

_____

GUIDE TO USING YOUR KEYS

"And I will give you the keys of the kingdom of heaven, and whatever you bind on earth will be bound in heaven, and whatever you loose on earth will be loosed in heaven" (**Matthew 16:19**).

The Bible uses a key as a symbol of authority. In Isaiah: 22:22, we see Eliakim the priest receiving "the key of the house of David… on his shoulder." Revelation: 3:7 uses similar symbolism. A trusted servant to the king wore the key to the king's house on a hook on his shoulder. Therefore, he had the authority to open or close the king's house. God has given you keys to open new opportunities in your life and to lock up obstacles that will attempt to stop you from achieving success.

Apply the 23 Keys. Study this list of keys every day. Make sure to use each one toward your plan of action. Do not skip any of the keys.

23 KEYS TO SUCCESS

Key #1) Pray to God.

Prayer comes before power. If prayer were a tool, it would be a hammer. It is your master key. The first thing to do when you rise in the morning is wake up your spirit with 1 hour of prayer. Make sure you pray about your daily activity towards your plan. Ask the Lord to bless every appointment and encounter you have.

Key #2) Have Faith in God.

Have faith in the plan God gives you. Do not allow doubt to enter your heart. Believe in the plan God has for you.

Key #3) Own Your Plan.

Make your plan personal. You are responsible for the success of your plan. The buck stops and ends with you. Give credit to the God in you for your ultimate success.

Key #4) Respect God.

Respect for the Lord is the beginning of success. Cherish His word. Read his word and speak it daily.

Key #5) Possess Character.

Be a good person. Exhibit the fruit of Spirit daily with love, joy, peace, longsuffering, kindness, goodness, faithfulness, gentleness, and self-control. Walk in the fruit of His attributes!

Key #6) Answer God's Questions.

When God asks, *What shall I do for you?* answer Him. Tell God what you need every day. Hear the voice of the Lord.

He is talking to you through His word, His voice, and the people and things surrounding you. He is constantly speaking to guide you!

Key #7) Know What You Possess.

What is in your house? Use the time, talent, and treasure God has given you to achieve your success. Triple T: TIME – Use it wisely; TALENT – It is in you; TREASURE – you have a measure of treasure and you can tap as much of it as you want!

Key #8) Be Open and Honest.

Whatever you have, God can work with it. Take a daily inventory of what you need to do, what you have to work with, and what you need help with. Walk in Humility!

Key #9) Go.

You are commissioned to follow the activity of your plan daily. Your steps are ordered of the Lord. Be flexible but not gullible. Put your plan to action. This is your salvation plan!

Key #10) Borrow.

Leverage what you need to progress. Do not be afraid to ask for what you need daily, even if you have to pay it back. Use these key phrases: investment, donation, loan, offering, and contribution.

Key #11) Invest in Vessels.

People are our greatest resource. Build up everyone you come in contact with daily with praise, compliments, and encouragement. Tell people about your plan!

Key #12) Fill the Empty.

Fulfill the assignment. Work to reach your goals by doing something toward them every day. This will bring a sense of fulfillment. Mark your daily milestones. Keep a calendar, log or planner.

Key #13) Come in.

Make and keep your daily commitments. Be dedicated to your plan. Always follow up your appointments, research, phone calls, etc.

Key #14) Shut the Door.

Stay focused on a daily basis; do not let anything or anyone distract you. Make your plan your first priority. Your plan is your future!

Key #15) Pour into Your Plan.

Perform tasks toward your goals every day. Let your actions speak louder than your words!

Key #16) Set Yourself Aside.

Dedicate yourself for service every day. Give your plan importance. If you're starting a business, think of a good brand name. What name has God given you? Walk in your God-given identity.

Key #17) Use Teamwork.

Enlist the support of others who can help you achieve your plan. Remember God is on your team. Do not be afraid to ask for help!

Key # 18) Proceed with Urgency.

Move quickly with strong intention every day. Do not put off what you can do today for tomorrow! You will see greater results.

Key #19) Obey.

Follow God's direction and instruction daily. You will see progress and production.

Key #20) Multiply.

Increase your profit. Be determined and focus your efforts to speed up productivity. Promote your plan daily through networking. Commission others to promote your plan by asking them to refer you!

Key #21) Go Sell.

Sell your idea, product, gift, or talent every day. Arrange to give or hand over something in exchange for money or trade. **ABC**: **A**LWAYS **B**E **C**LOSING your plan!

Key #22) Go Pay Your Debt.

It is only right to pay one's debts. Every day look for a way to alleviate your debt. Pay debts and forgive debts!

Key #23) Go Live on the Rest.

Live in abundant overflow with the revenue and rewards your plan produces. Enjoy the life God has created through you. Be in gratitude for what you have. Live in the lap of God's Luxury!

QUESTIONNAIRE

Where Are You on the Checklist?

Most of us experience setbacks of one kind or another in life. This list will help you to identify your current mindset. It is imperative to change your mindset in order to succeed. "And do not be conformed to this world, but be transformed by the renewing of your mind, that you may prove what is that good and acceptable and perfect will of God" (Romans 12:2). If you can relate to any of the scenarios below or know someone else in your life that can, please check the box beside the question.

Plagued by Problems?

- ☐ Do you keep trying and trying, but there is nothing to show for it but setback and despair?
- ☐ Have you tried plan after plan to be happy but nothing ever seems to work?
- ☐ Do you feel as if nothing is going to change in your life? It is just going to be failure after failure, so why even try?
- ☐ Have you stopped caring about what happens to you because you think you are a failure?
- ☐ Have you ever felt like you were going crazy and nothing in heaven or earth could stop you from losing your mind?
- ☐ Have you ever felt in your heart that nobody understands what you are going through?
- ☐ Are you afraid to trust anything or anyone in your life?
- ☐ Do you feel that no matter what you do, nothing seems to work and nothing matters anymore?

☐ Do you feel like the rug has been pulled out from under you one too many times and you just can't take it any more?

☐ Have you recently felt like saying, "I just quit, I give up?"

From Problems to Realizing His Promises

So often it appears that the problems in life outweigh God's promises. The truth is that His promises will help us to overcome our problems. "And you shall know the truth, and the truth shall make you free" (**John 8:32**). We are all blessed with the knowledge of the truth that leads to freedom.

☐ Have you ever felt you were destined for greatness?

☐ Are you ready to realize your true destiny?

☐ Are you searching for divine guidance to achieve greatness?

☐ Are you willing to explore the possibilities of no limits?

☐ How determined are you? Do you believe that nothing can stop you?

☐ Are you willing and ready to change your outlook on life?

☐ Do you believe God will take care of you?

☐ Are you ready to walk in freedom and abundance?

If you checked "Yes" to many of the questions on the list, then ***Seven Scriptures to Success*** is the answer for you. God is here to rescue you. He is here to move upon the Widow, the Fatherless, the Sorrowful, the Poor, and the Destitute. God promises He will never leave you or forsake you (**Hebrews 13:5**). He will always stay with us and provide for us.

TESTIMONY

"And they overcame him by the blood of the Lamb and by the word of their testimony" (**Revelation 12:11**).

Write down the testimony of your results.

Tell your rags to riches story. We would love to hear from you and share with the world the miraculous work God is doing in your life. We encourage you to send your testimony to our website:

AnthonyEcclesiastes.com

_____

_____

_____

_____

_____

_____

_____

_____

_____

_____

_____

_____

_____

_____

_____

_____

_____

_____

_____

_____

_____

_____

_____

_____

_____

_____

_____

_____

_____

_____

_____

_____

_____

_____

_____

_____

_____

_____

_____

_____

_____

_____

_____

RESOURCES

For additional resources and books from
Ecclesiastes International Publishing
visit:

AnthonyEcclessiastes.com

COMING SOON

P.I.M.P. For Life
(Positive Image Motivational Professional)

If (A Daily Devotional to Unleash the Christ in You)

Oil of Success

Knowing Who You Are

Children's Books
by Anthony and Christina Ecclesiastes

The Adventures of Zion the Lion and Israel the Lamb

When I Pray – The ABCs Of Prayer

Let's Have a Praise Party

I Am Blessed

God's Little Helper – featuring Ari the Dove

I Have The Spirit

I Can vs I Can't

I Am the Head and Not the Tail

Triple T's:

TIME – Use it wisely.

TALENT – It is in you.

TREASURE – You have a measure
of treasure and you can possess as
much as you want!

– Anthony Ecclesiastes

ABOUT THE AUTHOR

Anthony Ecclesiastes, President and CEO of Ecclesiastes Enterprises, is a pastor, community organizer, author, conference speaker, and multi-media personality. As a visionary leader with an entrepreneurial spirit, Apostle Anthony travels the world spreading the message of deliverance and freedom. He delivers a high-energy message that inspires people to shake off mediocrity and live up to their true greatness. Anthony's fields of expertise include: Mental Health Counseling, Financial Service, Law and Justice, and Business Coaching. He has been recognized as a top producer with major Fortune 500 companies. Anthony is a graduate of the University of Washington and the A.L. Hardy Academy of Theology. As class president at Atlanta University Center, he headed up the national student petition committee at the Martin Luther King, Jr. Center for Social Change to help establish Dr. King's birthday as a national holiday.

Apostle Anthony's life mission is to gather a prosperous harvest for the body of Christ. In 1994 Anthony began fulfilling his call to the ministry by serving as a pastor of churches in Eastern Washington. He has sent leaders all around the world, and has many spiritual sons and daughters teaching and preaching the concepts that God has shared with him. In 2007 he founded House of Wisdom, now known as Gathering the Harvest Tabernacle. Anthony lives in Bellingham, Washington, with his wife Christina and their children.

Apostle Anthony Ecclesiastes was born on March 17, 1961 in Savannah, Georgia, and raised in Springfield, Massachusetts. He was born to a single teenage mother to whom he credits his integrity, God-reliance, and early devotion to the gospel. At the age of 4, Anthony stopped breathing, and his young mother looked to God for supernatural guidance. She wrapped her baby in a blanket and took him three miles to the home of a brother and sister from the church. They prayed in the name of Jesus, and God raised the boy from the dead. Apostle Anthony is a living testament to God's miraculous healing power.